Copyright © 2021 Empower Your Life LLC

All Rights Reserved. No part of this publication may be reproduced or transmitted in any form or by any means, mechanical or electronic, including photocopying and recording, or by any information storage and retrieval system, without permission in writing from the author or publisher (except by a reviewer, who may quote brief passages and/or show brief video clips in a review).

Disclaimer: The Publisher and the Author make no representation or warranties concerning the accuracy or completeness of the contents of this work and specifically disclaim all warranties for a particular purpose. No warranty may be created or extended through sales or promotional materials. The advice and strategies contained herein may not be suitable for every situation. This work is sold with the understanding that the Author and Publisher are not engaged in rendering legal, technological, or other professional services. If professional assistance is required, the services of a competent professional should be sought. Neither the Publisher nor the Author shall be liable for damages arising therefrom.

The fact that an organization or website is referred to in this work as a citation and/or potential source of further information does not mean that the Author or the Publisher endorses the information, the organization, or website it may provide or recommendations it may make. Further, readers should be aware that websites listed in this work may have changed or disappeared between when this work was written and when it is read. Disclaimer: The cases and stories in this book have had details changed to preserve privacy.

Getting Out Alive: ISBN: Paperback 9781648731150 ISBN: EBOOK 9781648731112 Survivor Basics: ISBN: EBOOK 9781648731136 ISBN: Paperback 9781648731167 Initial Beginnings: ISBN: Paperback 9781648731174 ISBN: EBOOK 9781648731129 12 Step Guide to Restoration: : Paperback ISBN: 978-1-64873-228-7 ISBN 9781648731181 ISBN: EBOOK 9781648731143

Printed in the United States of America

Published by:

Writer's Publishing House

Prescott, Az 86301

Cover and Interior Design by Creative Artistic Excellence Marketing

Project Management and Book Launch by Creative Artistic Excellence Marketing
https://lizzymcnett.com

**National Domestic
Abuse Hotline
1-800-799-7233**

12- Phase Mind Power to Restoration

12 Phase Mind Power Workbook
By Purposed Survivor

Table of Contents

SECTION ONE 6

STEP ONE: 10

STEP TWO: 23

MIND POWER PHASE THREE: 40

MIND POWER PHASE FOUR: 51

MIND POWER PHASE FIVE: 77

MIND POWER PHASE SIX: 86

MIND POWER PHASE SEVEN: 96

MIND POWER PHASE EIGHT: 104

MIND POWER PHASE NINE: 114

MIND POWER PHASE TEN: 126

MIND POWER PHASE ELEVEN: 138

MIND POWER PHASE TWELVE: 150

PRACTICING THESE PRINCIPLES DAILY 160

Section One
The Twelve Steps

What is Restoration?

The purpose of restoration is simply to live free from the ramifications of domestic abuse. If you are willing to make an effort to find the solution to freedom, then these are the basic steps you must take to find freedom.

- We admitted we were powerless to our abuser- and the life we lived was unmanageable.
- We came to believe that a power greater than ourselves could restore us to sanity.
- We decided to trust the God of our understanding and then turn our will and our lives over to him.
- We made a searching and fearless moral inventory of ourselves.
- We admitted to God, to ourselves, and to another human being the embarrassment and humiliation

of our acceptance of the violence that retained our life.
- We were entirely ready to release and ask God to remove all of these imperfections of character.
- We humbly asked Him to remove our shortcomings.
- We made a list of all persons who harmed us, and became willing to make peace with our abusers and accept judgment is bestowed only by the god of our understanding.
- We made direct amends to ourselves and forgiveness statements to the people who have injured us.
- We continue to seek restoration through a daily personal inventory and accept responsibility for our actions.

Through prayer and meditation, we sought to improve our conscious contact with God as we understood Him.

In this process, we may encounter a spiritual awakening… one that will change the course of our lives forever.

Planning a life free from abuse is not something anyone should consider. Abuse of any kind is unacceptable. However, there are some questions you may want to ask yourself.

- Do you want to leave your abusive situation?
- Are you prepared for the difficulties of leaving?
- Have you accepted the abusive relationship and understand it's an unnatural way of life?
- Do you fully comprehend the results if you stay?
- Do injuries, violence, or even the fear of death plague your thoughts daily?
- Do you acknowledge the abusive situation changed you into someone you don't want to be?
- Do you participate in things because of physical force or threats?
- Do you believe you are a failure and the abusive situation controls every aspect of your life?

If you answer yes to any of these questions, then you have picked up the right book to read. Our fear of failure can eliminate any possibility of success if we let that frame of mind control our thoughts. It is never too late to admit you made a mistake and want to proceed with a better way of life. However, this decision takes determination to pursue a life filled with personal choices, ones that are not forced upon us by someone else. Only after we have made the conscious choice to escape our situation, can we truly find the freedom we seek. Any doubt can create an opening for excuses and denying the reality of your relationship. When you finally choose to craft an opening for the life you desire, commit to achieving restoration on the merit of terms you set for yourself, not for someone else.

Mind Power Phase One:

"We Admitted We Were Powerless to Our Abuser- and the Life We Lived Was Unmanageable."

Section One - Faith: What you are firm about in your thinking, you are firm about in your faith.

At first glance of the past, we may look upon it and see destruction or failure, and the idea of success or survival is hidden from sight. The fear, worry, and anguish have taken over every thought process we have. It's only at this time that we can truly see the light of day; our past and present must meet in the middle, so to speak, for clarity of our current fate.

Only after we recognize the reality of our situation can we acknowledge the outcome of our current way of life. If we continue in this fashion, there can only be an ending of sadness or death. Therefore, we must find the strength to leave. This is a point in our life, however, that the highest danger resides. But we must learn to acknowledge that the only way to find restoration is to leave.

Preparation for departure is not always an option, sometimes it occurs in the spur of the moment, and we rely only on instinct to guide us to safety. It's after we leave and the reality of our lives becomes clear that we pursue flawed reasoning why we should return. At these times, we must cease any immediate action and remain calm and never lose our purpose for the choice we made.

In this step, we learn the true meaning of strength, endurance, and persistence. Strength is more than just a physical characteristic, it's a state of mind in both health and conscious thought. People who suffer from many alignments are not always organically sick; their lack of strength comes from mental, emotional, or spiritual weakness.

By working through this step, we find the solution to where strength comes from and how we endured surviving in such turmoil. It's only after working through these steps that we can understand the nature of our existence. We begin to understand the problems we faced were not always of our own doing, nor were we to blame for the abuse we endured.

Each step is designed to guide us to restoration. Read and answer each question below with an open mind and honesty. Find someone to assist you if necessary, and be proud of the progress you have made in your life.

1. What does abuse mean to me?
2. Does my thinking follow a pattern?
3. Do I behave compulsively to avoid confrontation?

a. In what ways?
4. What thoughts do I act on without thinking of my actions?
5. Are these actions related to avoiding continued confrontations?
   a. Explain.

Denial

Often, we avoid the truth because it causes us pain and shame. When we deny the actions of our abuser, the strength we have gained is lost once again.

Acceptance is a part of healing and restoration.

1. Have I given plausible but untrue reasons for my behavior?
2. Are you in denial about being able to control my abuser's actions?
   a. Do I use the 'if I hadn't' excuse?
   b. Or 'if I had only done this before'?
3. Am I avoiding action because I am afraid of the shame I feel, or afraid of what might happen?

Hopelessness and Anguish

When we find ourselves in situations that are out of our control and there is no room for escape without injury, the time has come for a change. No relationship is ever open to abuse of any kind, mental or physical.

1. When did I realize my situation was hopeless?
    a. What led me to work through these steps?
2. When did I acknowledge staying was a mistake that could one day take my life?

Powerlessness

1. What does powerless mean to me?
2. Have I done things I am not proud of?
    a. List them.
    b. Why?
3. Am I nervous, fearful, and obsessive about avoiding conflict with anyone?
4. Do I apologize for any mistake I make?
    a. Is the possibility of abuse the reason?

5. Do I make every attempt to keep peace and create joy in all situations?

    b. Does panic set in until the situation has passed?

6. Do I immediately obsess about other incidences that might occur?

7. Have I lied or manipulated a situation to keep the peace and maintain order?

8. Have my decisions caused me or others pain?

Unmanageability

1. What was the deciding factor that led me to believe my life was unmanageable?

2. What does manageable mean to me?

3. Do I always give in to others, no matter the cost to my wellbeing?

4. Do I consider others' needs over my own to avoid confrontation?

5. Do I accept my role in an abusive situation?

6. Am I able to carry out my daily routine without fear of abuse?

    a. How has abuse affected my life?

7. Do I fake emotions to avoid conflicts?

    a. How has this affected my life?

8. Do I consider a day good if I avoid any form of abuse?

9. When in real danger, have I ever been indifferent to the situation or unable to protect myself?

    a. Explain.

10. Was this when I realized the severity of my situation?

Reservations

In any situation, we can find ourselves hesitant or unsure. These emotions are healthy and required for survival. It is only when we ignore these feelings that trouble occurs. We must recognize these reservations and acknowledge their existence. By admitting the apprehensions, we can move forward with the restoration of our lives. The feelings keep us aware of the past; they are a reminder of our abusive situation without hindering our healing process. These emotions will accelerate the process because we confess the awareness of our shame and embarrassment.

1. Have I accepted the full measure of my abusive situation?
2. Do I believe reconciliation with my abuser is possible?
3. Are there events that trigger my fears and worry?
4. Did I accomplish the task without undue stress?
5. What reservations am I still holding on to?
6. Am I afraid of other relationships for fear of abuse again?

Surrender

Surrender is a powerful word and can be used to greatly enhance our lives when we fully grasp the meaning. Strength comes from surrendering to the acceptance of our abusive relationship or relationships. The one mistake you don't want to make is just resigning to the abuse; in this case, you are not truly accepting the experience. Only when you can surrender and be at peace with the life you have lived can restoration begin.

1. What are my fears of surrendering?
2. What would my life be like when I completely surrender?
3. Will my fears subside when I truly surrender?
4. How can I go about surrendering?

Healing Practices

Have you heard of the expression that time heals all wounds? In some cases, this may be true, but not when it comes to abuse, mental or physical. There will always be damages that you do not fully comprehend or know about. Certain situations will occur and you may be caught with a completely unexpected reaction, for example, The deep stern tone of a man's voice, the pop of an aluminum can being opened, quarrelsome situations with family friends, or strangers, or even the simple act of having someone sternly tell you what needs to be done. These are just a few situations that you will face daily, so you must be fully aware of the manifested effects your abuse has had on your psyche. As stated above, you will never fully recover from the abuse, but you can find restoration and live a complete and happy life again.

1. Do I find myself dwelling on certain abusive incidences?

    a. Do I keep wondering how it could have been different, if only?

    b. Do I wonder if he were to get help, we could work things out?

    c. Do I find myself filled with hate or guilt, or uncontrolled emotions?

Strong feelings are a part of the aftershock of abuse, and it's normal to have emotional mood swings and uncontrolled outbursts from time to time. The mind, body, and soul are in a state of repair and healing. Embrace the emotions, and accept the healing process.

1. Do I have the urgency to discuss my abuse now that I am no longer residing in the chaos?
2. Does talking give me a sense of relief?
3. Are there parts of restoration that I have trouble believing?

4. Am I being open about my abuse with someone I can trust and talk with?
5. Are there parts of my abuse I keep to myself? Why?
    a. Have I written those circumstances down and dealt with the emotions they stir up?

The principal factor of this step is to acknowledge your powerlessness to your abuser. In order to accomplish surrender, you must keep your mind open and be willing to accept the abuse as a part of your past, and be ready to move forward with your restoration. Therefore, identifying that you're human and things happen, sometimes at no fault of your own, is a crucial part of healing. It's not where you were that matters; it's where you are going.

1. Do I have a sense that I am relative and important within my circle of friends and family or something in between?
    a. What is the sense?
2. Am I practicing the principles of this step daily?

    a. Explain how.

We must do more than just accept the abuse in our past to continue with a positive and successful future. The search begins with an inventory of the things that are hurting or angering us the most and then accepting those things for what they are. The next step is finding an organization with people who understand the trauma you endured and are willing to help you discover the dynamic individual you truly are.

    1. Have I made peace within myself?

    2. Have I made peace with the abuse in my past?

As you come to the end of this step, you may be wondering how did I possibly make it this far? The answer is strength. To evoke the power of your mind and body takes one simple method: elimination of doubt. Putting your faith in a higher power not only guides you to success, but also builds a strong mental character to withstand any future situations that may occur. Restoration is a personal choice.

    1. How do I move on?

2. How has my experience working through this step improved my life?

11. What is my understanding of the step?

To discover how we can survive a life without abuse, we must first understand the cause. Then we have to acknowledge the choices we made that led to the abusive situation. Remember, nothing changes if nothing changes.

Step Two:

"We Came to Believe That a Power Greater Than Ourselves Could Restore Us to Sanity."

Section Two - Strength: The word "strength" means "to endure," "to persist." Strength is the ability to keep on keeping on, despite negative conditions in a person's body or affairs.

William James described the power of faith as not only believing in a higher power but also power for your health. He said, "Faith is the habitual center of man's energies."

One of the first things you must do to restore health is to believe in a Higher Power greater than yourself. Sometimes when life steers us in directions away from a conscious contact with God, so we lose the ability to communicate regularly with Him. At this time, our lives become unmanageable.

If you are reading and starting to work through these phases it is because the life you have been living is not working. Avoiding any options that might say otherwise is denial in all its glory. We learn that faith is working all the time, no matter what is happening in your life. Your faith is the direct result of what you pay the most attention. Therefore, it is imperative to focus on what's good in your life and continue to manifest the best possible outcome for the future.

The following chapter is about faith and coming to believe in a power greater than yourself. Relinquishing any doubt or misgivings about what faith is or is not must be the first action. Starting this phase with a clear head, void of all preconceptions will allow your faith to grow in miraculous ways you cannot even imagine. Faith is probably one of the most powerful words in the English language. Simply saying the word, one can create incredible results immediately. Of all the 12 mind powers, faith is the only mind power that can overcome any circumstance in your life at this time. The first goal will be to understand the barriers you may face. The second is learning to identify what faith means.

By accepting abuse as a normal part of life, we acknowledge the lack of faith in ourselves. Accepting the past brings us to a new way of thinking. Once we acknowledge the abuse, it becomes part of our conscious thoughts. Awareness is necessary for healing our mind, body, and spirit.

The concept of hope has driven mankind for generations. It is the binding force behind our survival, the endurance to continue when all seems lost and no end is in sight. It gives us renewed optimism each morning.

When we chose this path, the idea of a better life did not seem possible, but HOPE is why we opened this book. Our renewed optimism came when we realized other people, just like ourselves, have progressed with purpose. Their lives are now based on meaning, not fear, and abuse.

1. What does faith mean to me?
2. What does it mean to have faith in a Higher Power?

Faithlessness

By accepting the abuse as a normal part of life we acknowledge the lack of faith in ourselves. Accepting the past for what it brings us to a new way of thinking. Once we acknowledge the abuse, it becomes part of our conscious thoughts. Awareness is necessary for healing our mind body and spirit.

1. Did I believe I could control the abuse?
    a. By what actions?
    b. Did these attempts work? Why or why not?
2. What things did I do that shame me now?

    a. Why do they shame me?

    b. Did I put myself in danger of doing these things?

3. Did I make excuses for my abuser's behavior?

    a. What were the excuses?

4. Did I ever over or underestimate my abuser's actions?

5. How was my life out of balance?

Hope

The concept of hope has driven mankind for generations. It is the binding force behind our very survival, the endurance to continue when all seems lost and no end is in sight. It gives us renewed optimism each morning when the sun rises.

When we entered this program, the idea of a better life did not seem possible, but the hope is why we opened this book. Our renewed optimism came when we realized other people just like ourselves have progressed with purpose. Their lives are now based on meaning, not fear and abuse.

You may not see proof of the hope for success at this point, but every time you get a realization about your abuse, the pain of that insight is accompanied by a surge of hope, making it possible to carry on with the next phase of your life.

Insanity

The question of unmanageability in our lives was never doubted. The problem became how do I stop it or get out alive? Many times, we were told, "just walk away," or "why did you get involved in the first place?" In most cases, if we had that answer we'd probably not be walking in these shoes. Our insanity is why we continued to remain as long as we did. There are no simple solutions to the problem. All we can do is continue to work on ourselves. Understanding our behavior and the reasons we made these choices will help us not make the same decisions repeatedly, which is the true meaning of insanity.

1. Did I believe I could control my abuser's behavior?
    a. How?
    b. Why?

2. What situations did I create to avoid additional incidences?

3. Did I behave in ways of which I am ashamed?

    a. What ways?

4. Did I make rash decisions to avoid conflicts with my abuser?

5. What kinds of requests did my abuser ask of me?

    a. Were they sexually-based?

    b. Were they things to humiliate me?

6. Was I ever forced to participate in things that I'm ashamed of?

    a. What?

    b. Why?

The dictionary defines insanity as, "a lack of reason or good sense, extreme foolishness or an act that demonstrates such foolishness." However, the basic concept of insanity is doing something repeatedly and expecting different results. The question you need to ask yourself is how insane was the true nature of your abusive relationship? Everyone has a different idea of insanity and it is unique to each person.

What some of us consider insane is a normal way of life for someone else, so, therefore, it's imperative we do not judge another person's life or choices. We must accept them for who they are and love them regardless of the decisions they make.

Insanity is a loss of perspective or a sense of proportion. In other words, our lives are out of balance. Gaining perspective on any situation requires a constant look at our daily activities. What do we place as important or priorities in our life? Each point has its meaning, you just have to decide which portion is the most important and remain vigilant in acting appropriately.

We can always choose a better way of life when we fill ourselves with love, compassion, trust, and hope. The conscious contact you can develop with your Higher Power will give all these things free of charge. You just have to be willing to accept them. When we've acted on an obsession, even though we knew what the results would be, what were we feeling and thinking beforehand?

1. What was my purpose to start?
2. Did the outcome meet my expectations?
    a. Why or why not?
3. Do I believe I acted appropriately?
4. What did I learn from the experience?

Releasing Faith

The previous discussion may have brought up numerous memories that are hard to accept or handle, but it is important to identify these memories and overcome the barriers that may prevent us from releasing faith.

1. Do I have any fear of coming to believe in a higher power?
2. Are there any barriers stopping my belief?
    a. What are they?
3. What experiences do I have concerning faith?
    a. Explain.
4. What do I believe in?

5. How has my faith grown?

6. What are my doubts about accepting a Higher Power?

7. Can this Higher Power keep me safe and free me from further abuse?

   a. Explain how and why.

8. What evidence is there in my life of a higher power?

   a. What are some things my Higher Power does for me?

   b. What are some things I must do to increase my faith?

9. What does a life of sanity mean?

10. What changes must I make to ensure my sanity?

    a. How must my thinking change?

    b. How must my behavior change?

    c. How have these steps changed my vision of sanity?

    d. How is restoration a process?

11. What are my expectations of sanity?

    a. Are they realistic or unrealistic?

12. Do I understand the restoration process?

13. Have I been able to maintain my sanity in unexpected situations that resemble my abusive situations?

    a. What were they?

    b. Can I go periods without feeling fear or trepidation?

14. How has it diminished or increased?
15. What are the circumstances that cause these feelings?
16. Am I over-reacting? Or do I have a valid reason to be fearful?

17. What must I do to stop these occurrences?

The Power of Faith

Each one of us came into this program with an entire life history. It is with these individual backgrounds that our level of faith varies dramatically, with one simple commonality: the abusive situation was a reality for all of us. This commonality brings a bond of familiarity for everyone, allowing each of us to accomplish the goals we set in our lives.

1. Why is having a closed mind harmful?

2. Am I willing to accept my past?

    a. Do I see myself as a survivor or a victim?

    b. Do I use being a victim as a way to gain sympathy from others?

4. Does this behavior allow me to deny the truth about the abuse?

    a. Do I believe that my abuser will ever feel sorrow for the abuse?

5. Does this allow me to deny my responsibility in the situation?

6. What change in my thinking am I willing to make for restoration in my life?

Restoration of Sanity

The word *restoration* is defined as, "the return of something that was removed or abolished." In this situation, the restoration is you; the ceasing of trying to be something you are not for the sake of someone else's misguided needs.

For your healing and spiritual growth, you must have a firm grasp on the meaning of sanity. This includes the continuation of rational behavior.

List some things you consider an example of sanity.

1. What changes in my thinking and behavior are necessary for my restoration of sanity?
2. What areas of my life need sanity now?
3. What steps can I take to ensure the sanity continues?

4. How will the continuation of working through the rest of these steps help in my restoration to sanity?

5. What changes do I see already in my life?

The changes in our lives are slow and gradual at times, and we may even wonder if all this work is worth the effort. As time passes and our restoration progresses, we will sometimes feel impatient or restless wanting an immediate fix for all our problems. This, however, is not possible. Restoration is a gradual process: it takes time and work. On the other hand, once you begin to recognize unrealistic behavior in your life it's a good sign. You are finally beginning to understand the meaning of insanity.

1. What expectations do I have about being restored to sanity?
    a. Are they realistic?
2. Is the progress I've made toward my restoration progressing as I have anticipated?
    a. Why or why not?
3. Do I understand restoration happens over time, not overnight?

Finding ourselves able to act sanely, even in a situation in which we were never able to succeed in the past, is evidence that our program is working in our life.

4. What instances have I encountered that fits the situation above?

   a. What was my feeling afterward?

Guided by Faith

One clear sign that we are guided by faith is the ability to make decisions with careful deliberation. We stop making rash and spur of the moment choices. Once the clarity of peace becomes a daily routine, our need for further restoration is a welcome change.

As you progress and develop a healthy faith in the God of your Understanding, you may become restless, even discontented with your life as it stands. This means faith is working to bring greater good into your life. This is the time to speak of faith and ask for continued guidance.

1. What actions have I taken to demonstrate my faith?

2. How has my faith grown?

3. Have I been able to move forward and make plans for my future?

4. Am I seeing the manifestations of faith in my life, no matter how small they may seem?

5. What fears are stopping me from moving forward?

6. What do I need to do to let go of my fears?

Spiritual Principles

The concept of restoration and living a life without abuse may seem foreign at this point, even impossible. It does not matter if you understand the power of God, the important factor is you believe restoration is possible. Faith will be the guide.

1. How do I trust the God of my understanding to release my fears?

2. Have I asked for help today from my Higher Power?

    a. Why?

    b. What for?

3. Have I sought help from others?

    a. Who? Why? When?

    b. Was I honest about my situation?
4. Did I try to manipulate their feelings in any way?
5. Were these manipulations used to get attention or approval?

Faith Revealed

As you come to the end of Step Two, understand that each phase of the process has its lesson and not all information will be revealed at once. Don't be discouraged if your progress is slower than you anticipated or not what you expected; the acknowledgment of faith is different for each person, as is the restoration of each person. Be patient, all will be revealed when the time is appropriate.

1. What is my understanding of Step Two, now compared to when I started?
2. What actions can I make to continue the restoration of my life after completing this step?

Step Three

Mind Power Phase Three:

"We Made the Decision to Trust the God of Our Understanding and Then Turn Our Will and Our Lives Over to Him."

Section Three - Judgment: The ability to understand our life and the choices we made.

The mind power of judgment is located in the stomach, which is the substance center of the body. Your stomach nourishes your body, just like your mind nourishes the soul. If you feed your mind with negative thoughts and malnourish your body, each center will act accordingly. There is no difference between the information, either good or bad. Therefore, keeping a positive attitude will nourish your mind and body with a life-giving substance.

Phase Three is what centers the mind and body to one frame of thought: the idea of surrender. You can accomplish almost anything when you surrender to the will of your Higher Power and release all past hurts, pain, and abuse. Remember, you cannot change the past, only learn from it and move forward with an open heart. The willingness to educate yourself on positive outcomes is a personal choice.

This process comes from time and patience, but not without work on your part. Restoration comes with the price of exercising sound mental practices. Working through these phases with an open mind and willingness to learn is one of the only obligations required for success. Your achievements rest solely on the motivation to change your life. The doubts and fears carried inside will only minimize your restoration.

We may find ourselves filled with the memories of our abusive relationship and afraid to commit to restoration because a fear of failure. This time, however, is unique in the sense that the decision to make this change is of your own doing. No one is forcing or controlling us to do something against our will. This one simple choice creates the movement for success. When we finally realize that freedom is possible and we can live free from abuse, our eyes are open, so we can begin to understand how wonderful life can be.

1. Can I make the decision today to move my life in a positive direction?

2. Does the idea of deciding cause me to be fearful?

    a. Why?

    b. **What are the fears?**

3. What steps have I taken or am I taking to follow through with my choices?

4. What areas of my life need to change the most?

    a. Why?

5. Why is it important to make these changes?

    a. How will these decisions make my life better?

Self- Will

Most of us came into this program believing that another human being was responsible for our happiness. We had spent much of our time pleasing them at all costs. When we could not please them, our first reaction was to torment ourselves with guilt, fear and worry. We'd then spent countless hours trying to figure out what we could do differently next time, and all the while our abuser manipulated the situation as they saw fit. With emotions that ranged from rage to tenderness, they became tornadoes whipping through the lives of everyone; while completely conscious of the path of destruction they left behind. If circumstances were not to their liking, they would try any means necessary to achieve their wants; they would get their way no matter the cost. Each of them was so aimed at aggressively pursuing their impulses any conscious thought was non-existent. This usually meant an explosive incidence, with human injuries and sometimes death. The context of this paragraph may be graphic, but reality can be harsh at times. To accept the past for what it is, the truth must be revealed.

The actions necessary to reveal the truth of our situation is something we must willingly to acknowledge and work on to surrender the past hurts. In doing so, we concede our self-will. They will center of the mind is a powerful force, and when left to work independently from the rest of our mental powers, it quickly takes control of every aspect of our lives. Self-will is a trait all humans have, and when exercised accordingly it can be a positive thing in our lives.

Will and understanding are the twin mind powers. They work harmoniously with each other, but only when we keep a close rein on the will portion of our mind power. The struggle to override our mind power of understanding is strong and can be difficult to control when not exercised regularly. This is a practice that will take time to comprehend. The dictionary states that will "is the part of the mind with which somebody consciously decides things, the power to make decisions, the determination to do something." It also states will "is the attitude or feelings somebody has toward somebody or something." These definitions have extremely powerful meanings and their explanations should not be taken lightly. Focus and clarity are the keys to understanding your will and God's will.

1. In what ways did I ignore my self- will?
2. How has not acting on self-will affected my life?

There are some fundamental elements to understanding the concept of self-will. The first is what you would consider important factors in your life. The second is what the true important factors are of your life. We come into this program thinking we are broken people who are not worthy of anything or anyone. This is simply not true. We are talented individuals who are seeking a happy existence without the threat of violence in everyday life. Our needs and wants should be met and achieved just like anyone else. Due to this fact, we become determined to gain the rights we deserve, sometimes at any cost. The price can be extreme when we are living in an abusive relationship.

1. Will pursuing my goals harm anyone?
    a. If yes, how?
2. In the pursuit of what I want, is it likely that I will end up doing something that adversely affects me or others?

3. Will I have to compromise any of my principles to achieve this goal?
    a. If yes, why?

God's Will

To understand the Will of God we must first comprehend the concept of giving. Will is the giving up of something and the acceptance of something else. In this case, it's the promise of a new life free from the clutches of domestic abuse.

The Will of God is for every human to live in the comforts of love and life. We can only accomplish this when we finally acknowledge the outcome is what we envision our lives to be. If we doubt a bright joyous future for our self, then that is what we will have. Doubt is only the outcome we can expect when our minds stay clouded with fear and uncertainty.

1. What is the difference between my will and God's will?

2. How can I learn to use my judgment to make better decisions?

3. Does the concept of a Higher Power scare me, or make me uncomfortable?
    a. Why?
    b. Explain.

4. Have I or do I believe God has caused or let these bad things happen to me?

    a. What things?

    b. Explain the reason for this belief.

5. What is my understanding of what God is?

6. How is my Higher Power working in the decision I make today?

Turning Over

The aspect of completely accepting the consequences of our actions is something all of us would like to ignore. Nevertheless, when we choose this path it blocks all chances of conscious contact with our Higher Power and learning to live by His Will is not possible. It is the conscious communication that gives us the guidance to live by His Will. This bilingual conversation is unique to each person, and the messages we receive are equally distinctive. This makes it imperative we learn to listen with an open mind to the answers we receive. Whether the solution comes in just a feeling, written words, or maybe a conversation with someone, the response must be accepted and the action should take place for any change to occur. The problem will resolve itself when we listen to the guidance of our Higher Power.

1. What does it mean to turn my problems over to God?
2. Are there parts of my life I'm fighting to release?
   a. What areas?
   b. Don't know how?

c. Can't let go?
3. Would the release of these things make my life better?
4. What do I need now to escape my situation?
   a. List them and be specific.
5. Will asking for guidance from my Higher Power release these problems I'm facing?
6. Do I need these issues or is fear keeping me from making the decision?
7. What decisions did I make with the help of my higher power?
   a. List them.

Faith Revealed

The passage of restoration depicts the progress of our faith and every area of life. We cannot pick and choose the areas we want to be restored and the ones we don't. To progress with the completion of our chosen freedom we must surrender to the Will of God and believe He will protect us in the future. Releasing faith is the common denominator between peace and confusion, or unjustified acts of insanity.

1. What portions of this step am I still struggling with?

    a. Why?

2. What actions do I need to take to overcome these problems?

3. What have I learned from working through Step Three?

Mind Power Phase Four:

"We Made a Searching and Fearless Moral Inventory of Ourselves."

Section Four - Love: Just as the heart equalizes the flow in the body, so love harmonizes the thoughts of the mind, bringing peace to both mind and body.

The next several phases are designed for the exploration of our character, and we learn to identify the exact nature of our wrongs. During the next section, you may find that your problems existed long before the abusive relationship started, maybe even as a child.

The mechanics of working through this phase will require an uncompromising inventory of past actions. Some memories conjured from listing your moral inventory may be disheartening and even painful, but the process can lead to the relief of pain, guilt, and shame. As long as you continue to carry the painful memories inside, restoration will be difficult.

If you have apprehensions about beginning this phase, it may be helpful to expel any misgivings or reservations about the difficulty of discussing the past. Turn your attention instead to the positive aspects and benefits of working through this phase. Then keep an open mind to what may be revealed..... Remember, the information disclosed is for your eyes only. This is a safe place, no one is here to judge you.

As a young child, depending on your upbringing, the concept of moral and personal values may have been foreign. Nevertheless, they are imperative to success.

Belief is having faith in a particular area of your life. In other words, what you value the most creates the environment in which you live. Whether it's money, sex, career, clothes, drugs, or power matters. You must decide what's important.

If your morals are based on solid spiritual principles, your life will be a success. If you dwell on the toxic memories, your life will follow suit.

Many of us have some type of morals or an idea of what values are, no matter how misconstrued they may be. The basic definition of morals is based on what somebody's conscience suggests is right or wrong. So, with this knowledge, your morals will change with whatever you focus on the most and consider important. In this case, working through these phases will help you establish a moral code based on spiritual principles.

1. Do I have any concerns about what this step might reveal about me?
2. What progress can I make by writing this moral inventory?

3. Do my issues and fears have valid backings?

    a. What are they?

4. Why should I be apprehensive about these issues?

5. Will admitting my faults or decisions re-build restoration in my life?

6. Am I working with someone to assist me with this step?

    b. Why? or why not?

7. Do I know someone who can help me?

    c. Make a list and state why I have chosen them.

Establishing Morals

Many of us have some type of morals or an idea of what values are, no matter how misconstrued they maybe. The basic definition of morals is based on what somebody's conscience suggests is right or wrong, rather than on what rules or the law says should be done. So, with this knowledge, your morals will change with whatever you focus on the most and consider important. In this case, working through these steps will help you establish a moral code based on spiritual principles.

1. Do I know what effect morals have on my life?
2. Do I know what it means to live by a moral code?
3. Do I understand these moral codes are what I value and not what society thinks?
    a. Do I stay in an abusive situation because of what other people might think of me?
    b. Have these fears compounded my feelings of hopelessness?
        c. Do I feel alone in this situation and like no one can help me?
4. Do I feel my situation is somehow my fault?
    a. Do I feel like staying in the abuse is the only way I can ever be loved?
    b. Do I believe I am an unlovable person?

c. Do I feel or have I been told I am worthless and deserve to be punished because of my actions?

   d. Have I ever been told I cannot survive alone?

   e. Have I been told I am too stupid to live alone?

   f. Have I been made to feel guilty for wanting to have a better life or live without being abused?

5. Do I believe my abuser's issues are my fault?

   a. Why?

   b. Where does guilt fall into these issues?

6. Do I understand what unconditional love means?

7. Do I believe love exists without physical abuse?

8. What does love mean to me?

An Inventory of Ourselves

This portion is designed to help us understand how the decisions we made affected our life. This step is not about other people, it's about us. Writing about your experiences with other people is necessary, but you must only look at your part in the situation.

The Inventory

Get a notebook, laptop, computer, or anything you want to use to write. Try to remove all distractions, especially electronic ones. Pray for guidance. Begin your list by looking at resentments, fears, behavior, beliefs, and secrets. Anything you can think of is inventory material.

Resentments

Some of us have struggled with finding fault in our part of the abuse. Rest your mind now, you are not in any way at fault for the abuse, although the decision to become involved in the relationship is another story. This is the reason for Step Four; it teaches us how to look at our part in any situation. The underlying factor is based on behavioral patterns. When you start to create a moral inventory of your life, the patterns develop a well laid out map. Taking images and experiences and putting them on paper will bring clarity to any situation. It prevents our minds from denying areas of the past that cause us pain. This is a survival mode in its finest glory.

This step is not only about acknowledging our behavioral patterns; it's also about recognizing the resentments we carry around with us. We can have resentments about anything that has to do with human society. They can be new or old opinions. Any emotion based on a feeling of being wronged or a sense of having been treated badly is resentment. We list these resentments to shed light on the reality of the experience or how we viewed the situation. Our view of the experience is important to our restoration process.

Since the old resentments have festered the longest it's best to start with them first. By acknowledging the past, it sheds light on the present, so many of these old resentments may be the cause of many of your current problems. They can manifest themselves in various ways. After listing all the resentments, you will begin to see behavioral patterns, and these patterns are the clues you need to proceed with the restoration process. The outline breaks down each little piece of the puzzle. You may be surprised to see the vast majority of these behavioral patterns are learned behavior from the past.

Your conduct and actions are a direct result of the environment you live in now. We are all products of our environment, whether we choose to be or not. The good thing is we don't have to stay products of the past. We can initiate the life we choose to live now. The actions we establish from working through these steps will create the solid foundation we need to be successful in anything we choose.

1. What people do I resent?

    a. Who?

    b. Explain.

    c. What is the reason?

2. Have I looked at my part and patterns in any of my relationships?

3. How has my avoidance contributed to these resentments?

4. How has my secrecy and silence developed these feelings of resentment?

5. Am I afraid of looking at these issues?

    a. Why?

6. Have my resentments affected my relationships with myself or others?

7. How has this affected my relationship with my higher power?

8. What recurring themes do I notice in my resentments?

Discovering Feelings

Our deepest desires are to be understood and loved as we need to be loved, not how someone else says we need to be loved. Examining our feelings in this section is done similarly to the way we analyzed our resentments. So many of us have buried our feelings deep down inside to protect us from being hurt, both physically and mentally, by someone we thought loved us. These feelings are buried so deep we may not even know what it is to feel joy, peace, and freedom. You may have had brief moments of these feelings, but most of the time they were predicated on when the sensation was going to stop! Those instances were filled with intense terror while we waited for the mood of the situation to change. Times such as these are the reason, we bury our feelings deep inside and rediscovering them can bring about additional trauma; however, the release will bring about healing and emotional stability.

You must find a safe space to continue with the next several sections of this step to ensure you get the most value from the experience and healing. Don't lose sight of the reason you started on this journey. The healing is in the feeling.

1. How do I discover who I am?
2. What part of my abusive relationship troubles me the most?
3. Have I shut my feelings off?
   a. What feeling do I fear the most?
   b. Why?
4. Have I denied the true nature of my abuse for fear of embarrassment or shame?
5. What situations cause my feelings to flood my conscious thoughts?
   a. What did I do to resolve the situation?
   b. How did my decision make me feel?
6. Was I working on old behavior and feelings when this situation arose?
   a. What have I learned after this experience?

Awakening Love

In this section, we discover how to release guilt, shame, and humiliation. It is estimated that 70 percent of all disease is caused by suppressed emotion. Regret, sorrow, and remorse tear down the cells in the body. Thoughts are the generators of actions. If these thoughts are not neutralized, they can create a deadly poison in the body that causes sickness and sorrow. Thoughts of love cause a beneficial chemical change to take place in the body. It brings forth life to renew health, and even change thoughts of death to thoughts of life. Just as the heart equalizes the life flow of the body, love harmonizes the thoughts of the mind.

1. What feelings of love have I created toward my past and present situation?
2. What feelings am I struggling to release?
   a. Why?
3. What steps have I taken to release these negative feelings?

Activating the mind power of love requires daily concentration to produce a positive love current. In return, these thoughts will break up and dissolve opposing thoughts of hate, guilt, shame, and humiliation.

When we were forced to survive in a situation filled with possessive limitations, it constricted our sense of freedom. This restriction brought about our feelings of shame and humiliation, along with the guilt we carried over thoughts of escaping our abuser at any cost. At times, the cost might entail bodily harm to our abuser, adding additional remorse. These feelings are normal survival impulses that are due to an abusive situation. You should not feel guilt over wanting to stay alive or free from harm.

1. Did I ever think of how to harm or injure my abuser?
    a. Did I ever wish they would die?
    b. How often did I think this?
    c. Did the situation ever get better?
    d. Did the abuse ever stop? If so, for how long?
    e. What caused the abuse to stop?

2. Was I ever severely injured or hospitalized?

    a. How many times?

    b. When? (Be specific)

    c. What excuses did my abuser give me?

3. What have you learned about your abusive relationship?

4. Do I consider abuse to be both physical and mental?

5. Is one or the other okay in a relationship?

    a. Is any abuse ever acceptable?

6. How would I describe my feelings toward my abuser? For example, Love, hate, fear, pity, numb, or don't know?

    a. Explain in detail.

7. How many abusive relationships have I been involved in? Include any family situations?

    a. Where did I meet them?

    b. How long did the relationship last?

    c. What is the status now?

8. Was the abuse from a family member?

    a. Who? And for how long?

    b. What did the abuse entail?

    c. Did I ever inform anyone?

Sexual Emotions

Discussing sex in any context can be uncomfortable for anyone, you are not alone. A large portion of the abusive relationship entailed sexual encounters that were both consensual and forced. Sexual intercourse is a personal act, one that is meant to be based on love and respect for the other person. When the sex turns cruel and abusive, our very nature is violated and we retreat within ourselves even further. The withdrawal is so severe at times it's like we have another person living inside of us, and both of them are fighting for control. These are all normal emotions after a traumatic event and your participation is nothing you should feel shame or guilt over.

The idea of discussing sex in any way can be uncomfortable. You may not even want to complete this section of the step, wondering how talking about your sexual encounters could help. But, for us to move forward with our lives we must understand the past and the choices we made. Cataloging the sexual encounters of the past is a reminder of our defects, especially if the incidences pertain to abuse from molestation, threats or physical force. Humans learn through repetition and observation. In other words, we are products of our environment. You must learn to be at peace with your sexuality. It will be the deciding factor in any future healthy relationships.

1. When was my first sexual encounter?
    a. With whom?
    b. Why?
    c. How long did it last?
    d. What are my feelings about the relationship now?
2. Have I confused sex with love?
    a. What were the results? How did that make me feel?

3. Have I ever used sex to avoid loneliness or to fill a spiritual void?

4. In what ways did I seek sex or avoid sex?

5. Is sex a prerequisite in my relationships?

6. What does a healthy relationship mean to me?

7. Do I think or believe I will ever have a healthy relationship with someone?

    a. If yes, when?

8. How should I proceed with this decision?
    a. If no, why?
    b. Give reasons.

8. What are some steps I can take to move forward before entering another relationship?

9. Why do I think these steps are important?

10. Do I think developing a relationship with the God of my understanding is important?

    a. Why?
    b. How can this help with future relationships?

11. How has the relationship with my Higher Power changed my life?

12. Do I ever feel I can love myself?

    c. Do I deserve to be happy?

    d. Why or why not?

13. What does it mean to love me?

14. What does it mean to love someone else?

    a. Does it mean to fear them?

    b. Does it mean to be a slave to their needs?

    c. Does it mean to be a sex toy?

    d. Does it mean to be abused, mentally or physically?

    e. Does it mean giving up your own life for them?

    f. Am I embarrassed or shameful of any of my sexual practices or any practices my abuser forced on me?

1. What are they?

2. When did they occur?

3. What are my feelings about the occurrences now?

Abuse

We must use extreme caution before working through this section. In fact, you may even have to postpone this portion till a late date. Use your sense of judgment before beginning this section. If you have any doubts, write them out and discuss them with a sponsor or life coach. The pain you may feel inside by working through this portion of this step can be unsettling if you are not expecting the outcome. In most cases, these incidences were caused by someone we trusted or thought loved us, and admitting we were violated in any way can be very painful. It is important to complete this step when you are ready. However, the secrecy of carrying this pain inside can cause continued destructive behavior. Confessing the truth of our abuse releases the pain and allows our mind and body to heal.

Abuse is never acceptable in any circumstance. We are not to blame.

1. Have I ever been abused (physically, mentally, emotionally)?

    a. By whom?

    b. When?

    c. How often? What was the duration?

2. Has the abuse affected my relationships with other people?

    a. How?

3. What steps do I need to take to be restored to spiritual wholeness?

    a. How can I ask my Higher Power to help?

4. Am I still plagued with memories of my abuse?

5. Is abuse the reason for my fear of developing new relationships?

    a. Why?

Assets

Many of us have spent a good portion of our lives looking or being told to look at our mistakes. When we only identify with the nature of our wrongs it can amplify the misgivings in our lives. This vantage point leaves us with a one-sided picture. Our lives have been filled with enough pain and anguish. Building good character traits begins with focusing on our assets.

1. What are some attributes of myself that I like?
2. What am I passionate about?
3. What do I think my purpose in life is?
4. How could I achieve that purpose?
    a. What steps would I have to take to discover my purpose?
5. What are 5 goals I have for myself?
    a. Can I create a timeline for these goals?

Finding Success

Moving from the past to the present requires one commitment: surrender everything to your higher power. Only after you have become willing and accepting can you achieve success in your life. Success is something you must seek; act and progress through each stage in your journey to restoration.

One method of finding success is to literally write out your plan, from beginning to end. The more specific you are about the achievements you want to attain, the greater your success will be. Another ingredient is to think big, and don't put limits on your abilities. With God all things are possible.

This portion of these steps is meant to be fun, so take advantage of the time. Objectively detailing your dreams and goals with good intentions will provide the success you desire.

Begin this section with two actual success lists. The first one should be a timeline detailing your restoration process. The second will be the list of your plans, dreams, and goals. Keep them simple to start, and make sure they contain doable accomplishments. This is meant to boost your self-esteem, not diminish it. Don't forget to include the success you've had getting this far on working these steps. This is quite an accomplishment and you should be proud.

Create a timeline of your success.

    a. Be specific.

    b. Don't fear success.

    c. Think big dream big.

Keep Your Goals for Success to Yourself
"When Someone Can't See Success for Themselves, They Can't See It for You."

Secrets

The message of this step is very revealing and should be contemplated before continuing. Is there anything you missed or skipped over because it was so bad that you can't possibly include it in your inventory? If yes, please understand you are not alone and keeping secrets is destructive to your restoration. The longer you hold this secret shows a lack of trust with your Higher Power and you have not fully surrendered. You are still living on self-will, not living by God's will.

1. Are there any other secrets I did not write in your inventory?

    a. What are they?

    b. Why did I not write about them?

If yes, you are not alone. Many of us have discovered secrets we just cannot reveal to anyone. In this case, write the account on paper, listing the details. After this, account all the aspects of the incidence and burn the paper. Release it to your Higher Power and let it rest, don't give the issue another thought. Time will reveal the necessary details when you are ready to handle them. Let trust and faith be your guide.

2. Can I write about them and share them with my higher power?

    a. Can I ask for guidance to resolve the issues?

3. Is any part of my inventory untrue or told to mislead someone?

Faith Revealed

Revelations of this magnitude can create many false misgivings. It is suggested that we at least discuss our feelings with our sponsor or life coach to make sure we understand the reality of our emotions. The past can creep up on us at any given moment and provide false information. Having a second opinion is always a great confirmation. Exploration of these emotions is important, if we don't dwell on them so much that they take control of our lives again.

The message of Step Four creates the initial beginnings of our restoration.

Mind Power Phase Five:

"We Admitted to God, to Ourselves, and to Another Human Being the Embarrassment and Humiliation of Our Acceptance of the Violence that Retained Us Life."

Section Five - Power: Every word brings forth after its kind--- first in mind, then in body, and eventually the affairs of the individual.

By admitting to God, ourselves, and another person the embarrassment and humiliation we feel for the violence that retained our life, we engage in the stages of restoration. Our admittance encourages trust in the restoration process. We can only live with the hope of restoration if the desire to achieve success is greater than the desire to remain in our current situation.

Our mind and body are connected as one unit. When abuse happens over time, the ramifications become reality. So, these traumatic situations create an adverse reaction with all parts of the body. The mind begins to create reasons for the abuse, as it compensates for the confusion, pain, and anguish caused by the situation. Without any new information, the mind uses past experiences to produce these ideas. In this case, the circle of violence continues in a repeating pattern until something causes a drastic change in reality. The alteration breaks the unyielding cycle of devastation, and a new transformation begins.

      1.   Do I have any reservations about this step?

2.   What are they?
   a. Explain.

Admitted to God

Our mind and body are connected as one unit, and what affects the mind affects the body. All these traumatic situations create an adverse reaction with all parts of the body. When the occurrences happen over a period, the ramifications become reality. The mind begins to create reasons for the abuse as a way of compensating for the confusion, pain and anguish caused by the situation. Without any new information to use, the mind uses past experiences to produce these ideas. In this case, the circle of violence continues in a repeating pattern until something causes a drastic change. The alteration breaks the unyielding circle of devastation and a new transformation begins.

1. Am I ready to talk openly with another human being about my abuse?

    a. Why or why not?

2. Have I prayed and talked with my higher power for guidance?

a. What help have I asked for?

b. Why?

To Ourselves

In our abusive situation the idea of forgiveness was not the center of attention, our survival was. Merely existing in these deplorable conditions was unthinkable most of the time and it became apparent that change was necessary for life to continue. However, finding a way to escape and "Getting Out Alive" did not seem possible until we opened our minds to release. It was the concept of change and hope that instigated an escape plan. Once these seeds were planted and the growth began, we were able to see a way out. The distraction was an ideal outlet, and it gave us a reprieve from the abuse. Hope was alive again and freedom became a reality. However, the thought of admitting the humiliation of our abuse can cause panic for many of us. We fear the ramifications of societal recourse, rejection, or additional humiliation. What we don't understand is that the admittance alone can bring us the peace we so desperately need.

1. Can I acknowledge and accept the exact nature of my abuse?

2. How will making this admission change the direction of my life?

3. Have I forgave myself for being abused?

4. Do I still feel shame?

    a. Explain.

5. Can I accept the abuse as a part of the life I lived?

6. How is learning to love me helpful?

7. Have I accepted every part of my body as God created me?

    a. Why or why not?

    b. Explain.

8. Have I accepted my current situation whatever it maybe?

    a. Do I understand everything changes and nothing stays the same?

To Another Human Being

Admitting the humiliation of our abuse can cause sheer terror for many of us. We fear the ramifications of societal recourse, rejection, or additional humiliation.

The nature of this next step is a process that may take some time to accomplish. The path to restoration is an individual progression for your life, not the life of someone else. Choose cautiously and carefully before picking a sponsor to share your admittance with. This will ease the discomfort you may be feeling.

1. Have I found someone to talk with?
2. Am I willing to talk with them now?
3. Have I openly spoken with this person about being a sponsor or accountability partner?
4. What fear do I still have about sharing with someone?
5. What qualities does the other person share with me?
6. Do they listen well?
7. Have they completed this step with success?

8. Are they compassionate about my fear?

9. How did I meet them?

10. Do they have any affiliation with my past abuser or old friends?

11. Do they know me and for how long?

12. Will they be biased and give me their honest guidance?

Releasing Faith

In this step, we must focus on self-honesty and commitment to the truth. It's an essential part of healing. We cannot grow by remaining in denial.

1. Do I feel the message of this step will improve my life?

2. In what ways have I developed the courage to work through this step?

3. Does my relationship with my higher power give me courage?

    a. Why?

    b. How?

4. How has working through this step increased my self-acceptance?

5. Can I begin to love myself?

6. What principles have I learned from this step?

7. Have I set a time and place for my fifth step? When and where?

Practicing self-honesty is an essential part of the restoration process and is the only way to find true happiness and freedom. These realizations are painful. However, if we channel our attention to other feelings that emerge through this process, we can wake to the promise of HOPE.

1. How have I avoided self-honesty in the past?
2. Does practicing self-honesty help me accept myself?
3. Have I been able to develop trust for another person through working this step?
4. How has my view of myself changed after working through this step?

5. Do I still have any reservations?

    a. What are they?

    b. Why?

We cannot grow remaining in denial.

Mind Power Phase Six:

"We Were Entirely Ready to Release and Ask God to Remove All of These Defects of Character."

Section Six - Imagination: The imagination is the scissors of the mind; you create the pictures, which take your thoughts and give them form.

We begin working through Phase Six, filled with relief and an idea of what freedom means. Our hope for a future without abuse is bright. We've seen the damage from our past and how it affected the present -- a glimpse of how we can begin to correct the issues. But first, we must be willing to have God remove our character imperfections.

In the process of working through the last five phases, we have started to discover the patterns in our behavior and learned how we are likely to act on the same imperfections over and over again. This awareness brings a conscious acknowledgment of our actions and the willingness to remove our imperfections of character. These imperfections are a creation of the past we endured. They do not make up the person we are inside. Our true nature is the total of our thoughts. The image you carry on the inside is what shines through for everyone to see. Patience and continual work are the keys to consistency and the only pattern that initiates complete restoration.

While we struggle through these phases and work on the new life we desire, the process can seem like a lifetime, especially when we face terrifying images and thoughts. Sometimes, it creates a false reality that leads us to believe we cannot survive on our own. This is false, an entirely ridiculous concept. The fear is what keeps us locked in this train of thought and minimizes our patterns of behavior. Unfounded fear remains long after the real situation has passed. Only by accepting our character imperfections and understanding why they have controlled our lives; can we begin the release and move forward.

1. Are there parts of me I like, but are afraid are my defects?
2. Am I afraid I'll turn into someone I don't like?
3. What defects do I think will be removed?

Asking for Release

How many times have you wondered what your life would be like without the abuse and constant life-threatening torture? The process of wanting things to be better and to live safe, free from harm daily is normal. A life filled with comfort and prosperity is a promised aspect of believing in a higher power.

1. Do I still believe in the process of restoration?
2. Do I believe in change?
3. How have I changed so far?
4. What are some things I want to change about myself?
5. How do I picture myself in one year?
6. Do I still have defects I don't think can be removed?
    a. What are they?
7. How do I think a higher power can help change my life?
    a. What openings can my higher power create for me to change?

Our Defects

Our process for removing our character defects in this step is much like the first two steps. The difference is, we now have a good idea of what acceptance and surrender means. When we were faced with the situation of an abusive individual, the concept of control was out of the question. Our entire life was surrounded by fear and an authoritative circumstance, which will eventually cause a termination of the person we were meant to be. We learn to suppress any emotion that warrants our continued abuse. This state of mind allows our survival instinct to run at full force. In doing so, our body becomes so accustomed to this flight or fight response, reality no longer exists in our lives. We become detached from our bodies. Our minds and bodies become separate entities, and as the abuse continues, we cloud all emotions completely. We must learn during this step to unlock that vault, to become vulnerable and ask these defects to be released.

1. How am I working to release or control the release of my character defects?
2. What is the difference between being entirely ready to have God remove my defects of character or suppressing them myself?
3. How is my trust increasing with God in this step?

4. What actions can I take to show my readiness in the release of my character defects?

The List

Character defects are the indicators of basic human nature. We will find as we progress in this program that we have the same basic nature as anyone else. These natural behaviors make us human. In these actions we make the same choices as others; these choices are based on needs, wants and sometimes desires. Future events are depicted by the actions we create because of our emotions. When we learn to maintain balance and consistency through the guidance of our Higher Power, our lives become manageable. Our goal is to raise awareness of our defects so that we can become entirely ready for their release. This is not done by analyzing their origin or indulgence in a bout of self-degradation. It is learning to accept the choice we made and stop hoping for a better past.

List each defect, and give a brief description. Then list the combatting the spiritual principle with its definition.

1. In what ways have I acted on character defects?

2. When I act on my character defects, how does it make me feel?

3. How do I associate these defects with certain feelings?

4. What spiritual principle can I use to counteract these actions?

Releasing Faith

Step Six is based on the willingness to change our thoughts about who we think we are. In doing so, we allow the true nature of our soul to be exposed. Committing to the restoration process is a continual pledge to the life we choose to live, not the life someone picks for us.

1. How am I demonstrating my commitment to restoration today?

2. Am I committed to my restoration?

3. What is the message behind Step Six?

The application of Step Six is simply the willingness to accept the person we are, no matter what we think our character defects may be. It is imperative to love yourself just the way you were created; that includes your mistakes and achievements. Any unwillingness to accept the past and acknowledge the future as bright and joyful will eventually paralyze our spiritual growth.

1. Am I willing to ask that all my character defects be released at this time?

    a. If not, why?

    b. When do I think I'll be ready?

2. What decisions do I need to make before I am willing?

The amount of willingness corresponds with the amount of faith and trust you have developed by working through these steps. We must learn to believe that our Higher Power will work in our lives to the exact degree necessary.

1. What level of willingness do I carry currently?
2. What level of trust and faith have I developed at this time?
3. Do I believe my higher power is working in my life?
    b. To what degree, and why?

As you progress in the restoration process your life will change dramatically. Feelings of uncertainty about your future may become overwhelming at times, even unbearable. But it is during these times that the most growth can be achieved with the right frame of mind. Learning to dream and create the life of our choice is something most of us did not ever imagine possible. Therefore, take this time to focus on the vision of what we choose to obtain in our restoration and maintain the vision during the rest of the process.

1. What do I see myself doing with the vision I created?
2. What type of career do I wish to obtain?

3. What will I do with my spare time?

4. What kind of parent, child, partner, or friend will I be?

   a. Be specific.

   b. Create a goal list.

Mind Power Phase Seven:

"We Humbly Asked Him to Remove Our Shortcomings."

Section Seven - Understanding: A peaceful state of mind brings about the solution to any problem. The calm mind heals.

The phases were designed to strip away the past, along with the aspects of your behavior and actions that led you to this outlet. As the parts of our life are peeled away, it raises awareness of each shortcoming and allows us to better understand the choices we made and why the results turned out as they did.

The understanding brings familiarity and even a serene calm because we finally realize the consequences of the choices we made. As this process takes place, we appreciate humility and surrender. We anxiously desire to be released from the dark images of the past and focus on spiritual principles. As this process takes place, we also gain a greater understanding of our faith.

1. When did I start to notice the calm settling over my life?
2. What healthy parts of me have surfaced?

3. What fearful portions do I still maintain?
4. How does knowing my fearful portions bring me peace?

Preparation for Release

This step is all about understanding the reality of our abusive relationship and the part we played. Granted we are not to blame for the abuse or the destructive situation, but our choice regarding the initial relationship and partner is an area of our life we need to address. We are masters of secrecy, silence, and manipulation of behavior, not for our gain, but our survival.

Step Seven may give us our first experience with feeling some sense of compassion for ourselves. We can make mistakes, forget something, or fail to get all our tasks for the day done and not fear an abusive situation. It's alright to be human and just take care of ourselves.

We can say no to something simply because it does not suit our needs. We can finally develop a connection with others, knowing that we are all subject to the same insecurities and failings as everyone else. We learn to accept our dreams and goals for the future as important. We are entitled to happiness, success, and prosperity.

1. How does accepting my humanity affect my restoration?
2. How does this knowledge help me accept who I am?
3. How has my relationship with my Higher Power improved working through this step?
4. How have the previous steps helped me work through this step?

Releasing My Shortcomings

To remove anything in our lives we must be willing to walk away, no matter what the consequences are. The giving up of something simply means to make room for your greater good.

Once you learn to develop an honest, sincere relationship with yourself, it will grant an opening for the release of any shortcomings that are limiting continual progress. When you can completely accept all aspects of who you are, your life will change in ways you cannot even imagine. These things include physical aspects as well as educational status, or financial situation. When you learning to center thoughts on your attributes, natural talents will allow you to become the incredible individual you were created to be.

1. How will I ask God to remove my shortcomings?
2. Can other people help guide me in this process?

Taking Action

At this point, you may be wondering how you are supposed to feel. This is a great question, because it is this feeling that will ultimately lead you to the restoration you desire. Discovery is the one key aspect of finding solutions. It is in these expressions that you perceive the power to see with your understanding. Seeing something is being able to understand. You do not see with your eyes as much as you see through your eyes, according to what you understand. Now the will to act according to what you understand is what will move you to the next phase of your restoration.

1. How will my surrender help to remove my shortcomings?

2. What are the benefits of letting my Higher Power work in my life?

3. How does it feel knowing God is working in my life?

4. Do I believe my Higher Power will remove my shortcomings?

5. Do I feel this release will give me the freedom I need in my life?

Releasing Faith

This is the point in our program that we may wonder how we are supposed to feel. We may find ourselves unsettled and struggling with certain aspects of our restoration, even our level of spirituality. These are all normal signs of restoration and becoming aware of our actions and emotions related to those actions.

In most cases, these experiences are clear signs of success, a continual desire to better ourselves: Seeking peaceful solutions to incidences that occur, making decisions in a calm state of mind without fear of physical harm or losing that constant feeling of having to please everyone in our life; basically, an overwhelming calm demeanor in every aspect of our existence.

1. In what areas of my life have I seen the most improvement?
2. What areas do I still struggle to release?
3. Have I developed a daily routine of prayer or meditation to relieve any fears or doubts I still have?
4. Have I written a gratitude list?
    a. Why or why not?

5. What accomplishments have I made working through Step Seven?

6. What shortcomings have been removed from working through this step?

7. What doubts do I still maintain after working through this step?

The following step was designed for our peace of mind and sanity, not our abusers.' The process will help us learn to develop relationships on trust, not fear. As you begin to prepare for working through Step Eight, remember forgiveness is the foundation of restoration and success in your life. Amends allow us to right the wrongs of our past. You must remember all these steps were designed to better your life, not anyone else's. It's okay to be selfish when it comes to improving your own life.

Mind Power Phase Eight:

"We Made a List of All Persons Who Harmed Us, and Became Willing to Make Peace with Our Abusers and Accept Judgment is Bestowed Only by the God of Our Understanding."

Section Eight - Will: If the will act is without the understanding, chaos will ensue in the mind, body and affairs.

We have come to probably the most challenging section, phase eight. The task of making amends with our abuser --- dealing with forgiveness.

The ability to forgive someone who has caused us pain, sadness, or bodily harm - intentional or unintentional - is one of the most problematic aspects of restoration. The harm inflicted was both physical and emotional. However, the mental can supersede the physical in many ways. The wounds and bruises heal, but the scars are left behind. These emotions are far deeper than we can imagine in some cases.

The concept of forgiveness is an act of complete renewal, washing away the hurt, and unveiling the new. It is a spiritual principle that should not be taken lightly. There should never be fear in forgiveness because it allows the release of old memories and their experiences. When you have been washed clean from the past, your divine plan can unfold as intended. The quicker you release and forgive, the sooner your greater good can be exposed.

You may feel that reviewing or writing about the abuse will cause you more pain, but it is the opposite. By clearing the actual abuse portion, it allows the pain, anger, guilt, and humiliation to release. This leaves your mind free to accept forgiveness.

Many people think forgiveness is for the other person….. it is not. The only person hurt by carrying the extra weight is you… "What you resist, persists."

1. You have been through a traumatic situation and healing takes time, so give yourself a break. How many times a day do you feel waves of doubt or bitterness?
2. Am I hesitant about working through this step?
    a. Why? Describe.

In this case, your reservations are valid. It is a big step that requires complete surrender for forgivingness to be possible. Forgiving is not something you just say, it's about how you feel.

Certain situations may require complete separation from our abusers. So, we not only face the anger of being abused, but we also have to face the anxiety of loss.

This is not unlike the loss felt over the death of a loved one. Grief can play a major role as well. Step Eight will guide us through the phases of resolving our forgiveness issues.

When you start writing a forgiveness record will be unlike any other statement you'll ever make. Your statement must be specific, entailing the details that encompass every hurtful word, the incidence of abuse, or the situation directed at you. The specific facts of the actions are not necessary: dates, times, duration, etc. Just begin writing this statement as if you were sitting across the table from your abuser. Explain why they hurt you, how it made you feel, and why you are angry. Be as honest as possible. Write the letter with love, understanding, and compassion. Remember, this statement is for you, not them. Don't give them any more control over your life than they already have.

1. List the people I am writing a forgiveness letter.
    a. Why those people?

The next phase of this step is accepting that we may never get any kind of amends from our abusers. The point of this section is not to hope for retribution or revenge. True forgiveness stems from love and prayer for their happiness. Bitterness and anger only destroy the life of the one who carries them around.

1. Can I let these resentments go?

    a. If not, can I add these names to the list and worry about the forgiveness statement at a later date?

Become Willing

Now that our list has been written, it's time to get willing to write the forgiveness statements. These statements must be from the heart and sincere. Otherwise, we will continue to repeat the same patterns. Promising ourselves we won't make the same mistakes again is not enough, because some of our behavior is so ingrained that we are not even aware of the effects it's had on our lives.

1. Why is it necessary to write a complete statement of forgiveness?

a. Isn't a list of names enough?

2. What if I can't forgive this person?

3. How can my Higher Power help with forgiveness?

4. What would my life be like if I'd already found forgiveness?

As you look at your list, images of your past may surface. Some of these pictures may not be so appealing, and many of them you've wanted to forget for a long time. Well, now you have the chance to do that. By releasing these instances with love, you create forgiveness statements that come from the heart. Believing you can find restoration on your terms allows the removal of these experiences.

1. Is there anyone I have not added to my list?

   a. Why?

   b. When will I add them?

2. Am I able to release the people on my list with love?

    a. If no, why?

3. What steps do I need to take to release them?
4. How can my Higher Power help me release them?

The focus of honesty, courage, and willingness to work on this step shows a true commitment to the life you have chosen to create for yourself. We must learn to forget about the resentments and blaming others for the choices we made. Accept our past, and stop justifying the excuses we have made for the life we led. We simply need to put these things on the list.

1. How does admitting the exact nature of my wrongs help in working through Step Eight?
2. Why is it so essential I be clear about my responsibility?
3. What are some examples of my honesty?
4. How does this correlate to this step?

We have already talked about making our list. The reason we need to write this list is how it can help our restoration and improve our life. Now, let's look at the reason we do not see at this point in our life. Our future is bright, filled with success, prosperity, and joy, but only if we are willing and able to let go of these resentments. When we bottle up this negative stuff inside our bodies, it creates health problems of all kinds, and it ruins our daily joy and any chance of ever having a healthy relationship with anyone. We will always be untrusting, spiteful, and leery of what might happen.

Developing intimate relationships with other people is what makes us grow into the people we are created to be. Sharing our hopes, dreams and desires with others is part of the restoration process. We can only keep what we have when we give it away. By maintaining resentments, we will continue to live a life of isolation, fear, mistrust, and secrecy; the one thing we have desired to flee. The choice is yours and yours alone.

1. Have I committed myself and my Higher Power to release these resentments?

    a.   Why or why not?

2. How many resentments am I still carrying?

    a. What are they?

3. Am I beginning to see how these resentments can ruin my chance for happiness?

    a. How?

    b. Why?

4. List the resentments I still have and their definitions.

Discussing every single one of these forgiveness statements with a trusted sponsor or friend is essential for you to receive the complete benefits of working this step. By sharing your feelings with another person, you will get a better insight into where your focus should be directed.

1. How do I feel about having to pray for willingness?

2. What are some things I've done to increase my willingness?

3. Have I made peace in my mind with my abuser?

    a. Why or why not?

5.   Have I asked my Higher Power to help me find peace?

When we've stripped away all the distracting elements of our abuse and exposed the solid core of serenity, humility, and forgiveness, we are ready for Step Nine.

Mind Power Phase Nine:

"We Made Direct Amends to Ourselves and Forgiveness Statements to the People Who Have Injured Us."

Section Nine - Order: Discern the difference between acknowledgment and acceptance.

The idea of being able to sit down and understand forgiveness is an incredible feat that should be celebrated. Due to the extent of our abuse, at one point the idea would have been out of the question. The point is that we come to a solution of mercy and compassion for another human being, even when they have wronged us.

As we begin the Ninth Phase it cannot be wrapped in a neat little package, or be disregarded as a minor phase, and accomplished quickly. This phase could take years to complete, or you may never fully finish it. When you are finally ready to write the forgiveness statements and focus on the outcome of each one, careful deliberation must occur to discern the consequences of that decision.

When we look at the decisions in our lives that created hurtful situations, the focus must be on the reasons our choice was made, not the abuse itself. Of all the phases, forgiveness takes the most discretion, because we must fully comprehend the past to move forward.

1. Has my trust grown enough to begin working through this step?

    a. If no, why?

2. How must I take the next step to improve my trust issues?

3. Am I ready to take forgiveness and make it a part of my life?'

Absolutions

Step Nine cannot be wrapped up in a neat little package to be disregarded as a minor phase and accomplished quickly. This step is something that could take years to complete, or you may never fully finish this one. When you are finally ready to write the forgiveness statements and focus on the outcome of each one, careful deliberation must be done to discern the consequences of that decision. We only make direct amends to such people wherever possible, except when to do so would injure them or others (especially ourselves).

When we look at the decisions in our lives that created hurtful situations, the focus must be on the reasons our choice was made. Therefore, making amends with careful deliberation is so important and we must keep the initial causes in mind.

1. What does amends mean to me?
2. What are some reasons I need to make amends?
3. How is making amends a commitment to change?

The changes occur slowly over time as we progress in our restoration. A guide to the process is how we feel about our self and the progress we've accomplished during the time we have worked through these steps.

1. What does progress in my feelings mean?
2. What part of these steps have I made the most progress in?
3. What portion of the steps do I still struggle with?
    a. Why?

Fear and Expectations

Sometimes we think rushing to get a result will alleviate the pressure we feel inside when in reality we only compound the problem. The superficial guilt and shame are what seems apparent, but there may be underlying issues we are not even aware of yet. These issues could be the initial cause of the decisions we made to enter an abusive relationship. Denial has kept the reasons at bay. It is only after we understand the repetitive behavior that clarity is formed and the real cause of our choices is unveiled. Unless we come to a complete understanding of the message taught by working through Step Nine. we are venturing into the unknown.

1. What does it mean to make amends to myself?

A difficult process to achieve is limiting your expectations of a particular situation. By assuming an expected outcome, you diminish the true purpose of the experience. The key is opening your mind to only positive results. As you begin to call on and release order in your life, everything in your world will respond positively.

1. What does it mean to have order in my life?
2. How does Step Nine require a new level of commitment to my program?

Establishing order is an emotional state of mind. First, you must be willing to stop the insanity that reigns free within you, minimizing anything that does not resonate in a calm orderly fashion. Stop making decisions based upon someone else's suggestions, concerns, or forced control over your life. These lessons are part of the process and restoration found in working through these steps. It's the awareness of the choices you must make that are important. Stop, look, listen, and then decide.

1. How have I begun to bring order into my life?
2. What are my concerns over trying to please people?
    a. Have I made any decisions that someone did not like?
    b. What decisions?
    c. How did I feel afterward?

3. How has the awareness of my emotions grown?

4. Can I accept suggestions from people without worry, stress, or fear of my choice?

Amends—Direct and Indirect

One of the most difficult amends you will ever make is to yourself. This makes it a priority that should not be ignored; release will come only when you are at peace with yourself. We have struggled with fear, and been manipulated by controlling behavior and rage. Even the consequences of our actions have brought us shame. In many cases, it seemed as though no matter what we did, it was not right or enough. We were always wrong.

Then after an extended period, we began to believe these lies, causing us to doubt every part of our lives. You took it so far as to justify the lies and excuses with plausible statements, and in certain situations, you may have found yourself defending the abuser. This action allowed them to blame you.

Manipulation of your feelings is a clear sign of a traumatic situation that could never end with a hopeful outcome. If you find yourself denying this statement, it's time to re-focus on the purpose of Step Nine.

The sole intent of the ninth step is meant to give a way and set right the damage of the past. In doing so, we grant our self-freedom, restoration, and a balanced relationship with us. We will simply be okay with who we are and the choices we made.

1. Have I ever made excuses for my abuser's behavior?
   a. When?
   b. Why?
   c. How did this make me feel?
2. Have I made excuses for my behavior?
   a. When?
   b. Why?
   c. How did this make me feel?
3. Has being honest about my behavior brought me peace of mind?

4. Have I accepted my behavior as part of my abusive situation?

   a. If no, why?

5. What are some additional steps I can take to continue the amends to myself?

6. How can the spiritual principles help me with making amends?

Some of us may have people on our list that we owe amends. If this is the case, the same process follows as the amends to you. Start with a letter of explanation concerning the exact nature of your wrongs. Keep in mind throughout our amends that the purpose of this face-to-face encounter is not how the amends are received or whether we receive amends in return for the harm done to us, it is about setting right a wrong. We are not making the amends to coerce or manipulate a reciprocal acknowledgment.

1. List anyone I need to make amends to. Include names

2. Are any of these people deceased?

3. Do I owe any amends that might have serious consequences if I made them?

    a. If yes, why?

    b. Who are they?

Making Amends

The process to prepare for such amends is done and you are ready to proceed with the task. If you are making amends in a face-to-face meeting with anyone you may be feeling as though you could walk on cloud nine, filled with relief and freedom from the guilt carried inside. Such a feeling could be a whole new experience for you and something to keep close to your heart. It is the first taste of freedom from the past. The work you have done is paying off. If you go forth with this frame of mind when you make your amends, chances greatly improve that your admittance will be welcomed.

1. Are there any amends with which I am having trouble following through?

2. What am I doing to reconnect with the reasons I need to make these amends?

The actual process of making amends is not always comforting. Our fears and doubts can well up and cause extreme worry or stress about the outcome or how we will be received. In this case, we must rely on our spiritual principles to guide us through the process and trust the outcome will bring the highest good for everyone involved.

1. What are my fears and doubts about making amends?
2. Are there any underlying issues I have not exposed yet?
3. What are my plans for re-committing to making these amends?
4. What can I do to follow through?

Faith Released

Step Nine gave us an outlet to finally let go of the past and acknowledge our portion of the damage. It is by our recognition and awareness of the damage that restoration will continue in life.

1. Can you make a list of the behaviors that you have forgiven yourself?

2. What are the benefits to me of practicing the principle of forgiveness?

3. What are some situations in which I've practiced this principle?

Freedom

The essence of Step Nine is relief of the guilt and shame. The concept of freedom is something we have been seeking for a long time. Our obsessive behavior that resulted from the abusive relationship is finally becoming clear, and we are now aware of the signs. The darkness in which we survived has passed and the freedom of a new life has begun. We can now begin to live with a fullness of heart and hope for the future.

Mind Power Phase Ten:

"We Continue to Seek Restoration Through a Daily Personal Inventory and Accepting Responsibility for Our Actions."

Section Ten - Zeal: A graceful, flexible attitude working within each person. Manifesting as great compassion and love.

The first Nine Phases led you to dramatic changes in your life. Some of them may be beyond anything you ever expected. We were able to conclude that our choices were not always accurate or successful, but we survived the situation. This path may not always be easy and free from problems, but with the knowledge we've gained, our tool kit is full and we are well armed to diffuse a situation before disaster can strike. As noted, this guide is meant to be a starting point, not the final word on any of the phases.

1. Why is Step Ten necessary?
2. What is the purpose of a personal inventory?
3. How can others help with my inventory?

Feeling versus Action

To begin the essentials of a personal inventory, we must first understand its importance. To keep what we have at this point, we must continue to practice the spiritual principles we have learned. You must learn to become more intimate with who you are as a person. This can be done by assessing patterns of behavior and doing a personal inventory. We must maintain a continuous awareness of what we're feeling, thinking, and even more importantly, what we're doing.

For example, if someone asks us, "How are you doing?" and we respond, "I'm terrible", the response comes from how we feel, not what we are doing. However, this response can have several meanings. So, we must be honest with ourselves and others about the true nature of the response. A daily inventory will solve this problem. It allows us to act on a situation before it becomes critical. Now, we may not always stop or prevent every situation, but we can control our behavior and emotions before, during, and after the fact.

By learning character qualities, we can control our behavior. Thereby, minimizing the way we react to certain stimuli. Our response is learned behavior, habits are what keep us in the same patterns. A written account is a conscious awareness of our actions, which helps alter the behavior.

All people are born with the ability to know right and wrong. However, in certain situations, we may have been forced to do things against our will, knowing it was wrong. As an instinct for survival, we participated in the event anyway, and now feel great remorse in having done so. We were living in survival mode and were reduced to an animal level. Our survival was essential.

The process of whether to make amends takes time, as many of us struggle to figure out what we did wrong. The choice should not be rushed or forced. Learning to trust our feelings and rely on intuition takes practice. The process will likely take the rest of your life, and it is not something you will ever perfect. It is part of being human. However, there is an inner peace you will develop deep inside; it cannot be mistaken once you learn to acknowledge it. The practice and completion of Phase Ten will help develop this insight.

1. Am I ever confused about my feelings, behavior, and habits or how they affect my life?
    a. Explain.

Understanding Right from Wrong

Most of us came into this program with a basic understanding of right from wrong. However, in certain situations we may have been forced to do things against our will, knowing it was wrong. As an instinct for survival, we participated in the event anyway, and now feel great remorse in having done so. Knowing the difference between right and wrong does not mean our emotions didn't take over the judicial process and we responded inappropriately. Thusly, our actions have caused extreme guilt and even shame in some cases. Before we came into this program, we were living in survival mode, and that means we were reduced to an animal level. We did whatever was necessary to survive.

1. What are some things I've done that I knew were wrong?
2. Have there been times when I was wrong and was not aware, I was wrong?
   a. What were they?
   b. How have I resolved this situation?
3. How do my wrongs affect my life?

Figuring out when to make amends can be difficult at times. Some of us may be wondering how to figure out if we did anything wrong in the first place. The choice is something that should not be rushed or forced in any way. Learning to trust our feelings and rely on intuition takes practice. The process will most likely take the rest of your life, and it is not something you will ever perfect. It is a part of being human. There is an inner peace you will develop deep inside; it cannot be mistaken once you learn to acknowledge it. The practice and completion of Step Ten will help develop this insight and give you the ability to rely on it. If you are truly stumped on whether or not you have done or said something wrong and need to make amends to someone, there are several options: 1) Locate the person and simply acknowledge that you may have hurt their feelings and you are sorry; 2) Write about the experience and pray on the situation; 3) Discuss the problem with your sponsor or life coach for advice. Whichever way you choose is solely up to you, but ignoring the situation will only compound the emotional trauma.

Unlike the previous steps, we have now moved onto living in the present and not the past. It is our first impulse to make an excuse or deny the choice we made. This doesn't excuse our behavior, because we are reacting to a potential conflict that may not even exist. So, we must begin to acknowledge our actions and promptly assess our decisions. Apologizing for the choices we make in our lives is no longer necessary.

1. What does it mean to me when I admit my wrongs?
2. Have I overreacted to any situations since I've been working through these steps?
    a. When?
    b. How did I handle the situation?
3. How did I feel after the situation was resolved?
4. How does promptly admitting my wrongs help me change my behavior?

Taking My First Personal Inventory

The key to changing any habit is consistency. Only through repetition can we alter our behavior. Changing a past behavior requires a minimum of 31 days with constant acknowledgment and exercising the behavior change. It does not matter if the behavior is good or bad, so you must be acutely aware of your actions daily. This is why we need a life coach or sponsor to help keep us guided in the right direction. As we continue down the path of restoration, these spiritual principles will become second nature, so to speak. You will learn to appreciate them and desire the progress and joy that they can bring into your life.

1. Why should I continue to take a personal inventory until it becomes second nature?

A Personal Inventory

The following list is some sample questions to ask yourself when you begin the inventory. Creating these lists can be used in any part of our life. It is advisable to consult your sponsor, life coach, or trusted friend for assistance with each step you are working on.

1. Have I reaffirmed my faith in a loving caring God today?

2. Have is asked my Higher Power for guidance throughout the day?

3. What have I done to be of service to God or the people around me?

4. What do I have to be grateful for today?

5. Do I keep a positive mindset no matter what is happening in my life?

6. What are some things I can do to achieve a better mindset?

7. Can I achieve success in my life without a God of my understanding?

8. How many times today have I consulted with my Higher Power before any decisions I had to make?

9. Did I feel good about the choice I made?

10. What happens if I cannot decide immediately?

11. Is it better to stop and think about my actions before reacting on impulse?

12. Do I continue to worry about the past, present, or future, and why?

13. Have I stopped to take care of myself today? Did I eat, sleep, and talk to someone?

14. What are some of the difficulties I faced today?

15. How did I handle the problems?

16. How did I feel at the end of the day?

17. Do I look forward to the coming day? Why?

18. What can I do to make my days better?

19. Have I continued to work on a future for myself today?

20. Do I have any feelings of guilt or shame about the day?

21. What did I do today that I want to repeat tomorrow?

22. Did I go to a meeting recently or talk to someone else in the program today?

Self-Discipline

In Step Ten, we learn the importance of self-discipline, honesty, and integrity with ourselves and others. The practice takes consistency and commitment to the future and the life we choose to live. Only when we truly commit to the actions of the present day can we achieve the goals we set for ourselves. At no time can we ever hope for a better past. All we can do is attempt to avoid repeating patterns.

1. Why is the practice of self-discipline necessary in this step?
2. How can this practice affect my restoration?
3. How do these practices change my behavior?

Keeping in constant integrity with our self is imperative for continual restoration. This state of being complete and undivided is how we maintain a set of high moral values.

1. What situations in my restoration have called on me to practice the principles of integrity? (Am I doing what I say I'm going to do?

   a. How did I respond?
   b. What decisions have I felt good about?
   c. Which have I not?

Faith Revealed

Along with working through Step Ten we have learned to admit our wrongs, and with such admittance came freedom unlike most of us have ever felt. Being whole is a state of mind that will eventually become something you desire daily. We've also learned that we are not inferior at all; we have just as much value as anyone else. Our life is important and we play a crucial role in the fabric of humanity.

1. How does this step help me to live in the future?

2. How am I living my life differently as a result of working through the tenth step?

The last portion of this step began to give us a glimpse of the future and what it holds. The freedom we obtain as a result of working through these steps gives us meaning and purpose. We find our thoughts are predicated on dedication and principles that improve our lives, not destroy it. We have the total freedom to create any kind of life we choose. Our success and prosperity rest solely on the actions we take from here on out. We have surrendered to being restored by our Higher Power.

Mind Power Phase Eleven:

"We Sought Through Prayer and Meditation to Improve Our Conscious Contact with God as We Understood Him, Praying Only for Knowledge of His Will for Us and the Power to Carry That Out."

Section Eleven - Elimination: The power of elimination is constantly infusing more energy into one's being while at the same time casting out of mind and body all waste. The forgiving love of our Higher Power is not only a wonderful spiritual stimulation for the soul and body; it is an important factor in the elimination process. Is causes an inrushing of the new as a letting go of the old takes place.

The Eleventh Phase is the search for inner enlightenment that develops a higher conscious contact with the God of your understanding. Along with this exploration, we will learn the concept of faith. The dedication will foster the means to your spirituality.

The conviction to seek spirituality is unique to every person. Only through prayer and guidance can we continue to grow, so whatever approach you choose, the process is personal and unique. Either way, the important factor here is that we continue the journey.

One aspect that is essential to healing is the law of forgiveness; it brings forth new life. When we surrender, it draws on the strength from God, the divine source. Therefore, old errors fall away, losing their grip on our lives. You must learn to accept the presence of new as the outworking of our restoration.

1. What disharmony have I felt in my life?

2. Have I experienced any enlightenment in my life since I have been working through these steps?

3. What presence in my life has my Higher Power shown me?

4. What does conscious contact with God mean to me?

5. How have I worked on letting go of the past to make way for the new?

    a. What have I let go of? Why?

    b. What am I still trying to let go of? Why?

6. How can I continue to develop my spirituality?

The conviction to seek out your spirituality is unique to every person. Some of us may need to take a new course, while others prefer to take the path they learned as a child and develop their family heritage. Either way, the important factor here is that we continue the journey.

Some of us get to this point and just don't know. Every path we have tried in the past has brought fear, doubt and/or resentments, and even the current avenues seem foreign. This is by no means a reason to get frustrated or discouraged. We all came into this program at different levels in our life. It's only through prayer and guidance can we continue to strive and meet our highest good.

While seeking to discover our spirituality, we are likely to visit spiritual institutions or community organizations. We are liable to read numerous books on spirituality and personal growth, as well as the people we will approach and meet during this journey. It is through this process that we truly discover who we are and our purpose. Whatever approach you chose, the process is personal and unique.

1. Do I know a specific path?

    a. Where did I learn this path?

    b. What are my feelings when I follow the principles?

2. What have I done to explore my spirituality?

Prayer and Meditation

One exercise that will develop a conscious contact with the God of our understanding is learning meditation or prayer.

The practice of prayer and/or meditation is as diverse as your spirituality. But the one basic model you need to form is a dialog. Relationships are a two-way street, and both parties must give to receive.

Prayer is talking to our Higher Power. It might not be through speech; it might be in our actions or the evolving feelings we carry. Either way, the communications must remain constant and progressive. Through the sequence of these phases, you have created a solid foundation to build on. Many of us have designated the process of prayer to specific times of the day, which helps develop good communication habits. These behaviors will also spill over into other areas, improving restoration in all aspects of your life.

1. How do I pray?
    a. Why?

2. What is my concept of prayer?

    a. Why?

3. When do I pray?

    a. When I'm hurting? When I want something? Regularly?

    b. Do I pray with gratitude?

4. How does it help to incorporate prayer throughout the day?

5. How does prayer help me to put things in perspective?

If this is your first experience at working through Step Eleven, you may be surprised that you have been praying and meditating during this whole process. Each time you participate in a meeting, meet with your life coach, sponsor, or sit in silence, you are evolving your conscious contact with God.

It is through this process we develop patterns of meditation. As stated before, meditation is as unique as the prayer process and spirituality. What you are learning is some guidelines to develop an understanding and knowledge of your Higher Power.

When you begin to meditate, try to minimize distractions, especially electronic ones, so you can concentrate on knowledge from your Higher Power. Our understanding of the communication we receive is not always a set of words or instructions; it may simply be a feeling or emotion. However, through regular prayer and meditation, it comes to us as a quiet sureness of our decisions and the lessening of the chaos that used to accompany all our lives and thoughts.

1. How do I meditate?
2. When do I meditate?
3. How do I feel about meditation?
4. If I have been meditating consistently for some time, in what ways have I seen changes in myself and my life as a result of meditation?

Conscious Contact

In a pamphlet written by Myrtle Fillmore in 1866, she recalls how her life was guided by a conscious contact with God. She states, "Life is simply a form of energy, and has to be guided and directed in a man's body by his intelligence.

How do we communicate with intelligence? By thinking and talking, of course. I can talk my way into live the life I desire. I began to teach my body and got marvelous results." As she projected the positive affirmations upon her body, the life energy began to grow and heal her illness as well as her soul. After being diagnosed with tuberculosis and six months to live, her body healed and she lived another 40 yrs. This is just an example of what the human mind is capable of doing when focused.

The concept of having a conscious awareness of God is not limited to certain beliefs, it simply means we notice or feel a presence in our daily lives. Faith does not come and go, or fade in and out. Our awareness is what comes and goes, according to our moods and deep feelings that constantly affect our conscious contact.

You do not live in your body as much as you live in the feelings and thoughts that envelop your body. This makes it imperative that we closely watch the attitude we have about ourselves and others. Learning to maintain a healthy relationship with our Higher Power serves to minimize the negativity that flows throughout our day. Meditation is a powerful tool to exercise and combat pessimism.

1. What are some things I can do to improve my mediation skills?

2. What is the importance of meditating daily?

3. In what circumstances do I notice my Higher Power?

    a. What do I feel?

God's Will

Deciphering the purpose of God's will is something we have all struggled with at one point or another. It does not always make sense and we can get frustrated trying to figure it out.

Part of this journey is we must work on to succeed in our restoration; it is in the searching that we find a conscious contact with our Higher Power. God's will bring an inner sense of peace that gradually spreads throughout the body, a sign that restoration is taking place. Once you have acknowledged this feeling, hold it close so you can recognize any variance in the future. This will help keep life in balance.

1. Have you developed a conscious contact with God?
2. How did I acquire this conscious contact?
3. Have I felt the inner peace that comes from having a conscious contact with God?
    a. When?
4. Have I worked to increase my contact?

Discovering Your Purpose Through Meditation and Prayer

The last portion of Step Eleven is learning how to decipher your true purpose in life. It is something we have all sought after. However, what most of us never realize is that our true purpose is already active, we just have to develop the skill to exercise it. Through constant prayer and meditation, the knowledge necessary to seek this information will be presented when the time is right. Only after you have found balance and peace in your mind can you be ready for your true purpose. There is a saying, "more will be revealed." This concept is based on living by the will of God, not yours.

As you continue to commit yourself to the restoration process, the balance you seek will come. The long-term results you desire to develop as your relationship deepens with the God of your Understanding.

1. How have I shown my commitment to Step Eleven and my restoration?
2. Have I prayed and meditated today?
3. Have I continued to pursue my commitment to my restoration process?

a. How?

b. When?

c. What have I done to pursue this commitment?

Faith Revealed

Our practices in this step show up in every area of our lives. As we continue to practice the principles we have learned, balance will be established, our sense of urgency will be released and we become secure in the process. Restoration is a journey, not a marathon.

We can finally become content with who we are, and satisfied with the life we have worked to achieve. Our focus can gradually switch to being of service to other Purposed Survivors, extending the gift of hope to them. This is when our true purpose begins to unfold in our lives. Freedom is upon us.

Mind Power Phase Twelve:

"Having Had a Spiritual Awakening as a Result of These Steps, We Tried to Carry This Message to Others, and to Practice These Principles in All Our Affairs."

Section Twelve - Life: Is one's state of mind. Call upon the power of life when the energy of human society drains your soul. Life is the gift of good mental consciousness.

The last phase of this book is essential to maintaining freedom. Mind Power Twelve is based on Life. So, if you are reading this sentence, then you have had a spiritual awakening. The nature of the awakening is unique for each person… regardless of the past.

The awareness of a higher power is something many people struggle with at first. But once the awakening emerges, individuals notice changes in their feelings. A spark will be ignited, allowing them to feel their purpose. Almost instantly, people will notice the growth. We still acknowledge accounts of the past and the importance of remembering them, but these experiences do not depict who we are anymore. Most of us feel we have a second chance at a new life. If you are still confused by the explanation, look at the small things….. sleeping at night, a feeling of peace, or thinking of the future.

The journey for us was not quick, but the painstaking effort we made transformed us into the joyous, vibrant people we are today. We look in the mirror and like the person we see. Recalling the past and looking at the way we lived is unthinkable.

Life has new meaning now, it's no longer something we just do. We remember that the expression of life is infinite. Dare to believe in the limitless possibilities for your future. Do not let inactive ideas clog your mind; rather, open your thinking to the awareness of a new life filled with creative ideas expressed through your affirmations.

    Repeat this often: *"My mind, body, and affairs are now filled and thrilled with rejuvenating life."*

This one simple affirmation can transform your mind, body, and affairs, bringing alive the natural energy already present in your body.

These phases are a foundation to help us restart life on solid footing; a concrete slab that we create for ourselves through honesty, integrity, and determination. Our ability to endure the experiences over and over again, while working through these phases, allowed us to see that we have the power and strength to survive any situation.

We may be looking back at this point and remembering friends, family, co-workers, whoever, wondering why they did not survive in the abuse. The thought is sad, and we may even feel angry, but through this spiritual awakening, we learn to accept that our Higher Power has a better plan for us and them. We have to acknowledge they are in a better place, free from further abuse.

The message of restoration can be broken down simply: *"Live free from abuse, restoration is possible, and there is hope."*

1. What is my overall experience of working through these steps?
2. What has my spiritual awakening been like?
3. What lasting changes have resulted from this awakening?

These steps are a foundation to help us restart our life on solid footing; a concrete slab that we create for our self, through honesty, integrity, and determination. Our ability to endure the experiences repeatedly while working through these steps allows us to see that we have the power and strength to survive any situation.

We may be looking back at this point and remembering friends, family, co-workers, whoever, wondering why they did not survive in the abuse. The thought is sad and we may even feel angry, but through this spiritual awakening, we learn to accept that our Higher Power has a better plan for us and them. We must acknowledge they are in a better place, free from any further abuse.

1. Have I been saddened by the thought of someone else's abusive situation?
    a. Who and why?
2. Have I prayed for guidance?
3. What steps have I taken to be of service to another Purposed Survivor?
    a. Who and when?
4. How did I feel about your decision?

Practicing These Principles daily

When we talk about the principles of restoration and practicing them in all our affairs, the key is "practice." These lessons cannot be achieved overnight and no one expects you to. We just need to keep actively pursuing the lessons daily. The spiritual benefits we derive from working through these steps depend on the effort you put in, not the success of the efforts.

Humility is most likely the greatest quality a person can carry. When we boast over our accomplishments and ramble about the success in our life, it sends a message of indifference to others. A program based on attraction does not come from success; it comes from the practical efforts of the people involved in the program.

The effective practice of managing all our affairs is not specific to this 12 Step Program; we cannot separate our career, relationships, or other areas of our life. Spiritual principles must be maintained in everything you do and everywhere you go. Integrity makes us who we are and what we stand for in life. Consistent prayer and meditation will help keep these boundary lines clear. Regularly attending meetings and meeting with your sponsor or life coach are additional ways to maintain integrity.

1. What are some areas in which I can practice the principles?

2. When do I find it hard to practice the principles?

    a. What am I doing to rectify the situation?

3. What principle do I have trouble practicing?

Setting Boundaries

One very important part of being a Purposed Survivor is anonymity. We must maintain a strict code of privacy for every person involved in this program, for our safety as well as theirs. By practicing the principles of unconditional love through Twelve Steps is essential. No one needs love without conditions more than a Purposed Survivor. Therefore, we don't ask anything of the people for whom we carry the message. We don't ask for money. We don't ask for gratitude, nor do we ask them to stay out of their abusive relationship. We simply extend ourselves.

This does not in any way mean we should not protect ourselves or take precautions. If we believe it isn't safe to bring the Purposed Survivor to our home, we should not. Practicing the principles of unconditional love does not require that we allow ourselves to be abused. Sometimes the best way to help someone is to stop enabling them and just pray for their restoration.

1. How am I practicing the principle of unconditional love with the Purposed Survivors I am trying to help?
2. How am I using my boundaries to keep myself and my family safe?

Often, we don't consider the effects our actions have on other people because we do not see the changes in person. The people could have been someone from our youth, a co-worker, friend from long ago, or just a stranger we met along the way. Each decision we make must be made with careful consideration not only for our life but for the people around us. Being absolute in our choices is not always possible, and we make mistakes or say things we don't mean. We are human. The important thing here is we handle the situation. Do you act appropriately and resolve any issues immediately, or do you keep the trauma inside, locking it away? The answer should be clear.

1. Have I practiced integrity with myself and others appropriately?

      a. If not, why? What was the solution?

  2. Do I plan to rectify the problem?

      a. When?

      b. How?

The issue of sponsorship is an important part of this program and your restoration. We carry the message, not for ourselves, but for the benefit of others. Finding joy in being of service is a crucial part of having a conscious contact with your Higher Power. The connection provides a way to remove the selfishness of our behavior and replace it with love and compassion for someone else.

Giving creates joy from which we can grow out of the fear of having to give under duress. When we see our efforts bring hope to another Purposed Survivor, the pain and abuse of our past were not in vain. This commitment ensures that we keep practicing the principles of our program, despite how we feel. Restoration requires a total commitment every day.

  1. Am I committed to my restoration?

2. What am I doing to maintain the forward progression?

3. Do I practice spiritual principles regardless of how I feel?

Practicing These Principles Daily

When we talk about the principles of restoration, the key is "practice." These lessons cannot be achieved overnight. We need to actively pursue the lessons daily. The spiritual benefits we derive from working through these phases depend on the effort you apply.

The effective practice of managing our affairs is not specific; we cannot separate careers, relationships, or other areas of our life. Spiritual principles must be maintained in everything you do and everywhere you go. Integrity makes us who we are and what we stand for in life. Consistent prayer and meditation will help keep these boundary lines clear.

1. What are some areas in which I can practice the principles?
2. When do I find it hard to practice the principles?
3. What am I doing to rectify the situation?

4. Do you act appropriately and resolve any issues immediately, or do you keep the trauma inside, locking it away? The answer should be clear.

Setting Boundaries

One essential part of restoration is practicing unconditional love for yourself. No one needs love without conditions more than a Survivor.

By practicing the principles of unconditional love, it does not require that we allow ourselves to be abused. Sometimes the best way to help someone is to stop enabling them and pray for their restoration.

We join society with excitement; the simplest little things seem easy. Our self-confidence brings poise when mingling with other people. Suddenly, our sights are set on living, not just surviving. If you wonder what's next, that is a positive attribute. Keep searching to find your answers. It is through this search that we discover the true meaning of our purpose.

You should feel proud of your accomplishment. The painstaking efforts of the work you achieved have opened the door for a second chance at life. Enjoy the freedom.

As we reflect on where we came from and what our restoration has brought into our lives, we can only find gratitude. Each one of us has something special to offer the world, and through this transformation, you have the ability and knowledge to pursue those interests with complete freedom. It's only with an attitude of confidence that we can achieve complete restoration.

How Will I Express My Gratitude Today?

Purposed Survivor Additional Books

- Getting Out Alive
- Survivor Basics
- Initial Beginnings
- 12 Step Guide to Restoration
- Get Hired – 30-day Guide to Finding a Job
- The Broken Angel
- IAM – A Guide to Self-Realization
- I'm Free – A Guide to Living Free

Follow us: @purposedsurvivor.com

www.ingramcontent.com/pod-product-compliance
Lightning Source LLC
Chambersburg PA
CBHW071455080526
44587CB00014B/2118